Santa's Favorite Office Jokes

*by Santa Claus
and His Helpers*:

Russ Edwards and Jack Kreismer

Editorial: Ellen Fischbein

Artwork: Jack Kreismer Sr.

Contributor: Angela Demers

Cover and Page Design:
Fred and Diane Swartz

RED-LETTER PRESS, INC.

Saddle River, New Jersey

INTRODUCTION

The holiday season in most offices is a very special time of the year. Christmas parties, secret Santas, decorations and even the occasional bonus all make the Yuletide merrier.

Now Santa's Favorite Office Jokes *can help carry some of that holiday cheer right on through the year.*

A treasure trove for any water cooler cut-up, these jokes are sure to keep a smile on your face even when the bills start arriving in January. To paraphrase the elves' cousins, the seven dwarfs, "I owe, I owe, so it's off to work I go." Ho Ho Ho!

Santa Claus

THE OFFICE PRAYER

Bless this office and all who toil within
Watch over your flock, forgive all the sin
From the white-lie gossip of office tales
To the whoppers that they tell in Sales

Office supplies pilfered in tiny amounts
And the wild-eyed padding of expense accounts
The office back-stabbing that diminishes us all
And faking a meeting so we can dodge a call

For doughnut gluttony and coffee abuse
And taking company vehicles for personal use
Oh Lord, forgive us all and grant our salvation
But if you can't, how about a four-week vacation?

The dour accountant entered the boss' office and announced, "I've got good news and bad news. The good news is that the IRS has agreed to have a heart."

"What's the bad news?" asked the boss.

"They want it by next Wednesday."

Q: Name the only man in history who was able to get all his work done by Friday.

A: Robinson Crusoe

Did you ever notice that boss spelled backwards is double s-o-b?

—Sanford Mims

A committee is a small group of the unqualified appointed by the unthinkings to undertake the utterly unnecessary.

—Fibber McGee (Jim Jordan)

Boss: Well, you seem to have everything a job candidate should have...and you've just gotten out of Yale. Now, what was your name again?

Job applicant: Yohnson.

Did you hear the one about the woman who made a fortune cleaning people's computers? Her slogan was "I do Windows."

D own at the stationhouse, a rookie cop hauled a little guy up in front of the sergeant. The man had a desk strapped to his back, was carrying a water cooler under his right arm, a typewriter under his left arm and was wearing a fax machine for a hat.

"What's the charge, Murphy?" growled the crusty old desk sergeant.

"Impersonating an office, sir."

J oe: The boss booked me on super economy business class for my trip to New York.

Moe: Super economy business class?

Joe: Yeah...There's no in-flight movie but they fly low over the drive-ins.

If you don't want to work you have to earn enough money so that you won't have to work.

—Ogden Nash

Work is of two kinds: first, altering the position of matter at or near the earth's surface relative to other matter; second, telling other people to do so. The first kind is unpleasant and ill-paid; the second is pleasant and highly paid.

—Bertrand Russell

"Son," said the old man passing control of the family business to his eldest boy. "The most important things in business are integrity and wisdom."

"How do you define integrity, Dad?" asked the young man.

"Integrity, my boy, is keeping your promises to the customers even if it means losing money."

"And what is wisdom?"

"Wisdom is knowing enough not to make those stupid promises in the first place!"

HO-HO-HO!

A t the office Christmas party, Bob was sitting at his desk fretting over some figures while the rest of the staff drank egg nog and generally whooped it up.

Spotting Bob, Harry went over to him and asked, "Gee, Bob. You look awful. What's wrong?"

Looking up from his figures Bob replied, "I've seen the ghost of Christmas Past—and it's shaped like a credit card."

I like my new telephone; my computer works just fine; my calculator is perfect; but Lord I miss my mind!

—Office Sign

*When my screen froze, the manual
suggested to reboot the computer.
So I kicked it again.*

—Randy Budnikas

Sales manager: So how's it going, Fred?

Fred: Well, I have bad news and worse news.

Sales manager: What's the bad news?

Fred: I only got three orders all week.

Sales manager: That's terrible. What's the worse news?

Fred: They were "Get out!", "Stay out!" and "Don't come back!"

Crumstead: I've been working here for fifteen years and doing the work of three people. I want a raise.

Boss: I can't give you a raise but if you tell me who the other two people are, I'll fire them!

The boss said to his secretary, "You're quitting after only five months on the job? How come?"

The secretary replied, "The reason will soon be apparent...and so will I."

Did you ever hear of a kid playing accountant...even if he wanted to be one?

—Jackie Mason

The biggest difference between genius and stupidity is that genius has its limits.

—Anonymous

"I made six figures in my previous line of work," said the job applicant. "I had a company car, a full health plan, dental plan, a five-figure bonus, a four-day work week in the summer, and eight weeks paid vacation," he continued.

"Wow," said the job interviewer. "How come you left the company?"

"They went bankrupt."

A calculator is a product you can count on.

A dvice to secretaries: Always proofread your work to make sure you don't words out.

Santa ordinarily finds cannibal jokes distasteful (pun intended), but if they're funny sometimes he'll let one slip by. Here's one such joke:

A cannibal chief captured a man and said to him, "What is your job?"

The guy replied, "I'm the editor of my company's newspaper."

"Ah," said the cannibal, "and soon you will be editor-in-chief."

Overtime: Time spent doing the work in the evening you never quite got around to during the day.

—John Kelly

An employer is someone who delegates all the authority, shifts all the blame, and takes all the credit.

—Anonymous

And then there was the salesman who inspired the bookkeeping department to create a whole new classification for his expense voucher: Accounts Deceivable.

"Why are you so late?" growled the boss.

"Well, boss...the alarm clock woke up everybody but me this morning."

"Waddya mean by that?"

"There are seven people in our family and the alarm was set for six."

The boss was invited over for dinner by one of his employees.

"Billy, why don't you say grace before we eat," said the employee to his son. "Just say the same thing you heard me say last night."

"Dear God," said Billy, "what ever made me think to invite my bumbling boss to dinner!?!"

People who live beyond their means should act their wage.

The trouble with unemployment is that the minute you wake up in the morning you're on the job.

—Slappy White

When more and more people are thrown
out of work unemployment results.

—Calvin Coolidge

HO·HO·HO!

The company had a successful year. The boss decided to go all out and have a catered Christmas party. He contacted the only chef in town, but since it was his busiest season, unfortunately the cook had to turn the job down. It seems he ran out of thyme.

Boss: Did you take any messages while I was out?

New secretary: Why, no...Are any of them missing?

ranchworth called all his employees away from their desks for the third time that week to have a meeting.

"Productivity around here is at an all time low," he began. Two hours later he concluded his harangue on the evils of malingering, which by now everyone knew by heart, and dismissed his employees.

As they filed out of his office, Branchworth called after them, "And we're going to keep having these meetings until we find out why nothing is getting done around here!"

The worst job I ever had was working in a Fotomat booth. I was the only one at the Christmas party.

—Mark Dobrient

A committee is a group of men who keep minutes and waste hours.

—Milton Berle

Did you hear about the employee who received a pay envelope without a check inside? He called the cashier and asked if his deductions finally equaled his salary.

Irving came back from lunch an hour late. His boss demanded to know where he'd been.

"Having my hair cut," replied Irving.

"On company time?" challenged the boss.

"Why not?" Irving countered. "It grew on company time."

"Not all of it," argued the boss.

"And that's why I didn't get it all cut off," answered Irving.

T he mayor's nephew was given a summer job painting lines on the streets of town. The first day he painted three miles of lines.

"Not bad at all," thought the supervisor.

The next day, the kid painted only two miles of lines.

"Well, everyone has an off day once in a while," rationalized the manager.

The third day, the nephew barely managed a mile of line and, political appointee or not, the supervisor decided to get to the bottom of the matter.

"What's the matter with you, kid?" barked the boss. "The first day you did three miles, the second only two miles and the third day just one mile. How do you explain that you paint less and less every day?"

"Geez boss, that's simple," the youth responded. "It's further back to the paint can each time."

Never hire anybody whose resume rhymes.

—Anonymous

OFFICE HOROSCOPE

Aquarius (Jan 20-Feb 18) The Water Cooler
Born under the sign of the water cooler, all your friends are richer from having known you. Perhaps you should consider staying out of those office football pools.

Pisces (Feb 19-Mar 20) Deskset
Things are looking up in your career. At the office, you're being exploited by more important people.

Aries (Mar 21-Apr 19) The Pink Slip
Your bonus this year will be up to six figures... Unfortunately they're the Board of Directors.

Taurus (Apr 20-May 20) The Copy Machine
It's time to think about giving up those three-martini lunches. They're beginning to cut into your cocktail hour.

Gemini (May 21-Jun 21) The Resume
(a lot of bull)
You have adopted a very successful career strategy. It's not whether you win or lose; it's how you place the blame.

Cancer (Jun 22-Jul 22) The Bonus
Around the office they consider you a true Renaissance Man. That's because you spend most of the time on your back staring at the ceiling.

Leo (Jul 23-Aug 22) Pencil Sharpener
You tend to get lost in thought...probably because it's such unfamiliar territory.

Virgo (Aug 23-Sep 22) The Coffee Machine
Your life is centered around coffee. In fact, you've recently discovered that you have too much blood in your caffeine system.

Libra (Sep 23-Oct 23) The Time Clock
At your place of business you are regarded as a member of the "in" crowd...incompetent, indecisive and incoherent.

Scorpio (Oct 24-Nov 21) The Briefcase
The gals around the office would place you in the "dark and handsome" category...It's gotta be pretty dark for you to look handsome.

Sagittarius (Nov 22-Dec 21) The Pay Check
You are the one who makes the wheels of progress turn. That's why you're known around the office as a crank.

Capricorn (Dec 22-Jan 19) The File Cabinet
Bad news on the career front. A year from now your income will be so low you'll be praying for jury duty.

A committee is a cul-de-sac down which

ideas are lured and then quietly strangled.

—Sir Barnett Cocks

Computer programmers snack on microchips.

Q: What did the navy captain say after he became a computer programmer?

A: "Don't give up the chip."

Interviewer: Why did you leave your last job?

Interviewee: Illness and fatigue.

Interviewer: Could you elaborate on that?

Interviewee: The boss got sick and tired of me.

Did you hear about the two computers who got married and had a baby? The first word it said was "Data."

A yes-man is someone who subscribes to the theory that it isn't who you know, it's who you yes.

—Anonymous

*My problem lies in reconciling my gross
habits with my net income.*

—Errol Flynn

The CEO of a match manufacturing company
receives a call from the president of the United
States. The president tells the CEO that he's going
to be given the Congressional Medal of Honor and
that he should report to the Rose Garden the next
day. The CEO has no clue as to why he should
receive such a distinction but he shows up the
next day at the White House. He's standing with
the president who, as the CEO is being presented
with the medal, says, "Terrorists tried to burn
down one of our most strategic military facilities
last week but their mission failed."

The CEO interjects, "But I don't understand,
Mr. President. What does that have to do with me
getting this medal?"

The president answers, "The matches wouldn't
light."

Husband: I was talking with the president of our company today.

Wife: Oh?

Husband: Yeah...he told me he was surrounded by "yes" men.

Wife: How did you respond?

Husband: I agreed with him.

It is no secret that organized crime in America takes in over forty billion dollars a year. This is quite a profitable sum, especially when one considers that the Mafia spends very little for office supplies.

—Woody Allen

A town solicits bids for a new city hall and the mayor has the top three contenders come into his office one at a time.

"Okay, Mr. Jones," says the mayor to the first bidder. "How much will it cost and how does your figure break down?"

"Two million," replies Jones. "A million for materials and a million for labor."

Jones leaves and the next bidder comes in and answers the same question.

"Four million. Two million for materials and two million for labor."

The mayor thanks him and he leaves.

Finally, Smith, the third bidder comes in. The mayor asks him how much the new city hall will cost and he says, "Six million."

"Six million?" sputters the mayor. "That's awfully high. How does that break down?"

"Easy," says Smith. "Two million for me, two million for you and two million for Jones."

Q: Why is it a good idea to have toast and coffee on the way to work in your car?

A: Because it goes so well with your traffic jam.

Two salesman are sitting at a bar in San Francisco.

"I read in the paper today that the president says that business is great and times have never been better," said the first salesman.

The second responded, "Oh yeah? Well, all I can say is he must have a better territory than I have."

I had a boring office job. I cleaned the windows in the envelopes.

—Rita Rudner

One of the best ways of avoiding necessary and even urgent tasks is to seem to be busily employed on things that are already done.

—John Kenneth Galbraith

"How do you get such great salespeople?" asked one company manager of another at a convention.

"Easy," replied his colleague. "It's our salesmanship training program."

"How's it work?"

"We send trainees out to try to rent an apartment. Once they manage to get a place, we put them in the field."

"So how does that make them a good salesperson?"

"When they knock on the door to talk to the landlords, they're carrying a tuba."

Lem: I'm not gonna go back to work unless my boss takes back what he said to me.

Clem: What did he say to you?

Lem: 'You're fired.'

Meek little Mr. Beamish shuffled into the boss' office, cleared his throat and said, "Mr. Jones, my mother says I should ask you for a raise."

"Very well," said the boss. "Tell you what...I'll go home and ask my mother if I should give you one."

If there was any justice in this world, oil-company executive bathrooms would smell like the ones in their gas stations.

—Johnny Carson

A study of economics usually reveals that the best time to buy anything is last year.

—Marty Allen

It was 5 a.m. when a beggar began knocking on a wealthy businessman's door. When there was no answer, he began banging relentlessly on the door.

Finally, the rich guy opens the door and says, "How dare you wake me up at this hour!"

The beggar shouts back, "Hey, I don't tell you how to run your business so don't tell me how to run mine!"

Boss to elderly employee: You know, you've always been shy. Now what I'd like you to be is retiring.

A nd then there was the company that discontinued all its employee physical fitness programs after it determined that its workers got all the exercise they needed jumping to conclusions, flying off the handle and beating around the bush.

N ext time you're putting on your necktie as you get ready for work, think about this: Does it make any sense to start off the day tying a little noose around your neck?

Retirement at 65 is ridiculous. When I was 65, I still had pimples.

—George Burns

When ordering lunch, the big executives
are just as indecisive as the rest of us.

—William Feather

During the pre-employment screening, the company psychologist wanted to check the applicant's grasp on reality.

"Now tell me, son," began the shrink. "If you looked out that window right now and saw a battleship coming up the middle of the street what would you do?"

"I'd jump in my submarine, fire a torpedo and sink it."

"Where would you get the submarine?"

"The same place you got your battleship."

HO-HO-HO!

You know the years are piling up when bartenders at the office Christmas party start checking your pulse instead of your ID.

Riley was meeting with an important client in the conference room when he decided to look important so he got his secretary on the intercom and said sternly, "Miss Johnson, please get hold of my broker."

Tired of her boss's orders, Miss Johnson replied, "Of course, Mr. Riley. Is that stock or pawn?"

Hard work never hurt anyone who hired somebody else to do it.

—Jay Kaye

It is better to have loafed and lost than never to have loafed at all.

—James Thurber

"I've developed a computer that's almost human," said the inventor.

"Can it think like a human?" asked his trusty assistant.

"No, but when it makes an error, it blames another computer."

Harry: I see you've lost some weight since you started your new job. Did your boss put you on a diet?

Larry: Nope, he put me on commission.

An accountant at a big income tax service could hardly stay awake at his desk and his yawns finally prompted a rebuke by his boss.

"Hamilton, what's wrong with you anyway? It looks like you've been burning the candle at both ends!"

"Sorry, Boss," answered the CPA. "But I had insomnia last night."

"Didn't you try counting sheep?" inquired his boss.

"Yes, sir, I tried that but I made a mistake and then it took me all night to find it!"

If work is so good for you, how come they have to pay you to do it?

—Sanford Mims

Most employers are in the novelty

business these days. It's a novelty when

their employees work.

—Anonymous

"How come you're an hour late this morning, Riley?" demanded his boss.

"It was so slippery outside, that for every step I took, I'd slip back two."

"Well, then how did you manage to get here?"

Riley responded, "I finally gave up. I headed back for home."

The company doctor agreed that medical people spend far too much time on paperwork. Now he just has his caddy keep score for him.

Two executives meet for lunch at an exquisite eatery.

Farnsworth: How's your investment portfolio doing?

Dibshank: Not so good...It's my broker.

Farnsworth: What's wrong with your broker?

Dibshank: Let's put it this way...The only securities he's concerned with nowadays are maximum, medium and minimum.

You can know a person by the kind of desk he keeps...If the president of a company has a clean desk, then it must be the executive vice president who is doing all the work.

—Harold S. Geneen

There are 365 days per year available for work. There are 52 weeks per year in which you already have two days off per week, leaving 261 days available for work. Since you spend 16 hours each day away from work, you have used up 170 days, leaving only 91 days available. You spend 30 minutes each day on coffee break that accounts for 23 days each year, leaving only 68 days available. With a one hour lunch period each day, you have used up another 46 days, leaving only 22 days available for work. You normally spend 2 days per year on sick leave. This leaves you only 20 days available for work. We are off for 5 holidays per year, so your available working time is down to 15 days. We generously give you 14 days vacation per year which leaves only 1 day available for work and I'll be damned if you're going to take that day off!

—Author unknown

A salesman parked his car right under a "No Parking" sign and left a note on the windshield. "I've circled this block 25 times and I have to make an important meeting or lose my job...Forgive us our trespasses."

When he returned from the meeting, he found a ticket on the windshield. On the back it read, "I've circled this block 25 times and if I don't write this ticket, I'll lose my job...Lead us not into temptation."

A nd then there was the less than stellar businessman who thought Dun & Bradstreet was an intersection.

SANTA & CO.

No man goes before his time...unless the boss has left early.

—Henny Youngman

Business Cards

Who says business people can't be funny – business people? Consider some of these signs and slogans from the world of commerce...

ON A WATCH AND CLOCK REPAIR SHOP:
IF IT DOESN'T TICK - TOCK TO US!

BEAUTY PARLOR SIGN: CURL UP AND DYE.

SIGN OUTSIDE THE PERMANENTLY SEALED
REACTOR AT THREE MILE ISLAND:
GONE FISSION.

ON AN OBSTETRICIAN'S BUSINESS CARD:
WE DELIVER!

IN THE WINDOW OF A MUSIC STORE:
GUITARS FOR SALE. CHEAP.
NO STRINGS ATTACHED.

WINTERTIME SIGN OUTSIDE
A MINNESOTA NUDIST CAMP:
CLOTHED FOR THE SEASON.

THEN THERE'S THE VOODOO SCHOOL
WHICH ADVERTISES:
HEX EDUCATION.

SHOE STORE SIGN: COME IN AND HAVE A FIT.

SIGN ON THE DESK OF
THE HEAD ENGRAVER AT THE U.S. MINT:
THE BUCK STARTS HERE.

ALTHOUGH HE NEVER HAD IT PRINTED
ANYWHERE, THERE WAS THE DERMATOLOGIST
WHO'D TELL ANYONE WHO WOULD LISTEN THAT
HE BUILT HIS BUSINESS FROM SCRATCH.

OF COURSE, THE LADIES FLOCK TO THE
PLASTIC SURGEON WHOSE CARD READS:
DROOP THERAPY.

Guidelines for bureaucrats: (1) When in charge, ponder. (2) When in trouble, delegate. (3) When in doubt, mumble.

—James H. Boren

Overheard at the water cooler:

Chuck: Hey Stan, how come I never see you on the golf course anymore?

Stan: Oh, I gave up golf for bowling.

Chuck: Bowling? How can bowling possibly be better than golf?

Stan: Well, last night I bowled for three hours and never lost a ball.

Did you know that one of Santa's reindeer works for Procter and Gamble?

Comet cleans sinks.

A nd then there was the elderly executive who was so old that when he chased his secretary around the desk, he couldn't remember why.

Q: What kind of munchies are computers hooked on?

A: Microchips

Coffee is a pretty powerful stimulant.
I had a friend who drank twenty cups
a day at work. He died last month, but
a week later he was still mingling in the
company lounge.

—Milton Berle

Boss: The man at the office who's late when you're early and early when you're late.

—Anonymous

The head of the sales department winced as his new assistant gave a report to the Board of Directors.

"This has been a really cool job. I was afraid that it was going to be lousy but it turned out really cool. The last time I did something like this it was lousy but the people here are cool and so I was surprised at how cool it turned out when it could have been totally lousy."

After the meeting, the sales manager took his young assistant aside and said, "George, there are two words I don't want to hear you use in the future. One is cool and the other one is lousy."

"Fine," replied George. "So what are the two words?"

T hen there was the guy with a B.A., an M.A., and a PhD. The only thing he didn't have was a JOB.

This is a story about four people named: Everybody, Somebody, Anybody and Nobody. There was an important job to be done and everybody was asked to do it. Everybody was sure somebody would do it. Anybody could have done it, but nobody did it. Somebody got angry about that, because it was Everybody's job. Everybody thought Anybody could do it but Nobody realized that Everybody wouldn't do it. It ended up that Everybody blamed Somebody when Nobody did what Anybody could have done.

—Author Unknown

*By working faithfully eight hours a day
you may eventually get to be boss and
work twelve hours a day.*

—Robert Frost

A guy goes into a bar and orders a martini. He then pulls a jar out of his pocket and sits it in front of him. He finishes the martini and puts the olive in a jar. He orders another martini, drinks it and puts the olive in the jar. He repeats this over and over until the jar is full. He screws the cap on the bottle, puts it in his pocket and staggers to his feet.

"Excuse me," said the bartender to the martini man. "But that's the strangest thing I've ever seen."

"What's so strange buddy?" asked the tipsy patron. "I work for a restaurant and the boss sent me out to pick up a jar of olives."

"Well, that's it," said the young man on the phone. "I've quit my job and I'm now officially a full time writer."

"Oh really?" said his skeptical mother. "Have you sold anything yet?"

"Sure. Lots of things."

"Like what?"

"Like my car, my stereo, my watch..."

Boss: Hard work never killed anybody.

Employee: Yeah, but when's the last time you heard of anyone who rested to death?

What's right is what's left if you do everything else wrong.

—Robin Williams

Contract: The large print giveth and the small print taketh away.

—Anonymous

Personnel Manager: We pay 125 dollars a week.

Job Applicant: That's an insult!

Personnel Manager: We only pay once a month. That way you won't be insulted so often.

Two guys were talking about a mutual business acquaintance. "He used to work for me," said Bosworth. "If you're going to have any business dealing with him, you'd better be on your toes."

"Are you sure?" asked Finster.

"Positive. I taught him everything he knows."

" Joann, will you marry me?" proposed the grandfather clock manufacturer.

"I'm afraid I can't, Bentley. My father told me to never hook up with a clockmaker."

"Why's that?"

"He said you'd always be working overtime."

W aggenheim entered the office building lobby on a gray, dank Monday morning. Hank, the elevator operator, smiled and said, "Have a nice day."

"Sorry," the disgruntled executive said as he stepped out of the elevator. "I've made other plans."

Happiness: When you wake up in the morning and see your boss's picture on the milk carton.

—Ken Polish

Bert worked for Conglomo Enterprises for forty years. Each evening he would leave his office with a box tucked under his arm and bid a good evening to Farnsworth, the watchful security guard. After several decades of this, it was time for Bert to retire and, as was his habit, he walked through the lobby precisely at five with a box tucked under his arm. When he got to the security station, Farnsworth stopped him.

"Bert, I heard you retired today and I have something to tell you. Every night I've seen you go out of here with a box under your arm that you didn't have when you came in. It was driving me crazy so we inventoried the office supplies time and again and nothing was missing. We also accounted for every piece of stock, equipment and even toilet paper. I know you've been stealing something and it's been extremely frustrating to me. Bert, we've known each other for a long time and I won't be seeing you again. Just between you and me, what have you been pilfering all these years?"

Bert smiled and patted the package under his arm as he answered, "Boxes."

Mrs. Biddle hadn't seen Mrs. Banks for several years when one day they happened to meet on the street. Mrs. Biddle asked Mrs. Banks, whose husband was a draftsman for a contracting company, how his career was going.

"Oh, he's still drawing," answered Mrs. Banks.

With a trace of a sneer, Mrs. Biddle asked, "Unemployment or Social Security?"

Sign in an office: "We shoot every 3rd salesman and the 2nd one just left."

No problem is so big or so complicated that it can't be run away from.

—Linus (in "Peanuts")

Bulletin Board Graffiti

I SLAVE AT THE OFFICE.

DID YOU EVER FEEL THAT YOU WERE A
TYPEWRITER, WHILE EVERYONE ELSE IN THE
WORLD WAS A WORD PROCESSOR?

TODAY IS THE YESTERDAY
YOU WORRIED ABOUT TOMORROW.

I CAN'T COMPLAIN, BUT SOMETIMES I STILL DO.

WHEN THEY SHIP STYROFOAM,
WHAT DO THEY PACK IT IN?

MISERS MAKE LOUSY RELATIVES
BUT GREAT ANCESTORS.

BAD COFFEE IS GROUNDS FOR DISMISSAL!

TODAY IS THE FIRST DAY
OF THE REST OF THE WEEK.

IF YOU'RE GOING TO DO ANYTHING, DO IT WITH
TOTAL COMMITMENT...AT LEAST SOMETIMES.

DEATH IS LIFE'S WAY OF TELLING YOU
THAT YOU'VE BEEN FIRED.

IF YOU CAN KEEP YOUR HEAD WHILE THOSE
ABOUT YOU ARE LOSING THEIRS, CONSIDER A
CAREER AS A GUILLOTINE OPERATOR!

*The worst thing about retirement is having to
drink coffee on your own time.*

—Joe Dolan

*A conference is a gathering of important
people who, singly, can do nothing but
together can decide that nothing can
be done.*

—Fred Allen

Whacker went in to see the boss about a raise and after stating his case the executive replied, "Well, Whacker, at this time, given the surfeit of qualified personnel for your position in the employment marketplace and factoring in the termination of certain governmental tax abatement policies towards our industry as well as the highly variable fiscal projections for the third quarter and allowing for your own professional performance profile, it would prove injudicious for any officer of this firm to commit to either a salary increment or to any other enhancement of a personal benefits package."

Whacker was lost. "Huh? I don't get it," he said.

"Exactly," replied the boss.

The business owner called his lazy son into his office and said, "Look, kid, it's about time for you to assume some responsibilities around here. Which part of the business would you like to take over?"

"Well, I don't like sales. I don't like administrative work. I don't care for public relations..."

"Now, kid, I'm making you a full-time partner. You gotta tell me what you want to do."

"Since you asked, Dad," replied the son, "I think, most of all, I'd like for you to buy me out."

He who builds a better mousetrap these days runs into material shortages, patent-infringement suits, work stoppages, collusive bidding, discount discrimination- and taxes.

—J.E. Martz

The closest to perfection a person ever comes is when he fills out a job application form.

—Stanley J. Randall

Conversation by the water cooler:

"By the way, Joe, how long have you been working here?"

"Ever since they threatened to fire me."

Hal: I don't like drinking coffee at work.

Sal: Why's that?

Hal: It makes me toss and turn at my desk all day.

Gertrude: My boss is such a slavedriver. The stress is unbelievable. My blood pressure is sky-high, I get migraines every day. My doctor tells me I'm a candidate for a heart attack or a stroke if I keep this up.

Lily: So what keeps you from quitting?

Gertrude: I have a terrific health plan.

Skinflint boss: Please don't tell anyone what I'm paying you.

Disgruntled employee: Don't worry. I'm as ashamed of my salary as you are.

Before I had kids I went home after work to rest. Now I go to work to rest.

—Simon Ruddell

Simms, fresh out of Harvard with an MBA, sat across from the personnel director brimming with confidence as he figured he had pretty much aced the interview.

"Tell me, what were you looking for in the way of a starting salary?" asked the personnel director.

"Oh," said Simms, "A hundred fifty thousand a year with stock options."

At that, the personnel director said, "Of course, you'll also be getting a luxury company car, six weeks paid vacation, a full pension after six months, a secretary, a personal assistant, your own private washroom, an unlimited expense account and a year-end bonus equivalent to ten percent of the company's earnings."

Simms couldn't believe his ears and blurted out, "You must be kidding!"

The personnel director replied, "Of course I am but you started it."

The company's boss had his personal assistant write all of his speeches. His assistant was so good that, after a while, the boss didn't bother to read them before speaking.

At the firm's semi-annual meeting, the boss was at the dais delivering a motivational speech. He reached the bottom of a page which read "And this brings us to two critical points..." The boss turned to the next page only to find the words: "I quit. You're on your own now."

Did you hear about the guy who quit working for Weight Watchers? He heard the chances for promotion were slim.

If at first you don't succeed, keep on sucking till you do succeed!

—Curly Howard

I am a friend of the working man and I
would rather be a friend than be one.

—Clarence Darrow

"Sir," said the underling office employee to his boss, "can I take a day off next week to go Christmas shopping with my wife?"

"Absolutely not," snapped the boss.

"I knew you'd be understanding. Thanks for getting me out of it."

Then there was the newly appointed federal agent investigating illegal computer activities. He promised to take a big byte out of crime.

One day the boss was approached by a longtime employee who began working for the firm when his grandfather started it decades before.

"Sir, I wonder if I might have a word with you?" the old man wheezed. "Coming up the beginning of next month is my 50th anniversary with the company and I was just wondering if I could have the day off to celebrate with some old co-workers up at the retirement home."

"Well, all right," growled the boss, "but don't go expecting this every 50 years!"

A salesman is a fellow with a smile on his face, a shine on his shoes, and a lousy territory.

—George Gobel

Corporation: An ingenious device for obtaining individual profit without individual responsibility.

—Ambrose Bierce

Then there's the guy who hands out blank business cards. He wants to remain anonymous.

Art: How's your business?

Bart: It's a non-profit organization.

Art: I didn't know that.

Bart: Neither did I until I found out I couldn't make any money.

Personnel Manager: And just what are your job qualifications, young man?

Job Applicant: I have a Ph.D. from Yale where I graduated number one in the class. I was voted Most Likely to Succeed in both high school and college. I've authored six books on business and sales, each one of them a bestseller. And I've just sold my own investment firm for a cool ten million dollars.

Personnel Manager: That's quite an impressive story. Is there anything negative about you at all?

Job Applicant: Just one thing...I'm a pathological liar.

The meek may inherit the earth, but it's the grumpy who get promoted.

—Father Francis Mulcahy, "M*A*S*H"

*Outside of traffic, there is nothing that
has held this country back as much as
committees.*

—Will Rogers

A secretary said to one of her colleagues, "I finally managed to make the boss laugh."

"How's that?"

"I asked him for a raise."

"I'm going to mix business with pleasure," said the boss to his lazy employee. "You're fired."

"Our feather company changed its mascot from a goose to a duck," said Harry.

"Sounds to me like you're downsizing," said Larry.

A nd then there was the one about the traveling computer salesman who remembered his hardware and software but forgot his underwear.

T wo secretaries were talking about computers over lunch.

"With word processing," said Sally, "I can now type one hundred words a minute."

"Yes," answered Bernice, "but you can also erase that many pages in a second."

Voice mail is the technological upchuck of the age.

—Herb Caen

My husband was so ugly, he used to stand outside the doctor's office and make people sick.

—Moms Mabley

The secretary buzzed Mr. Oberman on the intercom. "There's a call from the Big Boss."

"Oh my. Oh good heavens! Let me take a few deep breaths...Alright, put it through."

When the call was connected, Oberman managed a very nervous, "Hello, sir, and what can I do for you today?"

"Well you can pick up some milk and bread on the way home, but you don't have to call me 'sir'," replied Mrs. Oberman.

Sign on fence—Salesmen Always Welcome... Dog Food Is Expensive!

The whole network was down. Simpson was frantic at the sight of all his employees sitting idly by, waiting for the computer repairman to arrive. When he finally did, he observed that the monitors were dark, the memory was scrambled and the main CPU was overheating.

The repairman calmly strolled behind the machine, took out a rubber mallet and gave the console a tiny tap in the middle. Instantly, the system rebooted, the monitors all came back to life and the computers were fully functional.

The repairman then stepped up to the boss and said, "That'll be one thousand dollars."

"One thousand dollars!!!" the boss screamed. "You weren't even here a minute and you're asking for one thousand dollars? You're crazy...I'm not paying a cent until I get an itemized bill."

"Okay," sighed the technician, whipping out his invoice book and jotting down his itemized bill. It read, 'Wear and tear on mallet from tapping computer- 20 cents...Knowing where to tap it, $999.80.'

Rule number one: The boss is always right. Rule number two: If the boss is wrong see rule number one.

—Author Unknown

Two efficiency consultants talking:

"The other day I did a study of my wife making my breakfast. I counted her steps, monitored all her movements and noted all the deficiencies in her work habits."

"Did you cut down on the time it takes to fix breakfast?" asked the other efficiency expert.

"Yes, now *I* do it in half the time."

Did you hear the one about the jingle writer who applied for unemployment?

He filed a claim because he had to work under ad verse conditions.

I make money the old fashioned way. My salary's the same as it was 10 years ago.

I like work; it fascinates me. I can sit and
look at it for hours. I love to keep it by me;
the idea of getting rid of it nearly breaks
my heart.

—Jerome K. Jerome

Work is the tediously slow dragging of
fingernails on the blackboard of life.

—Russ Edwards

As he finished installing the new computer work station at Frisbee's desk, the technician told the clerk, "This little baby will do half your work for you."

"Great!" said Frisbee. "Then install another one."

Barton: I had an awful accident yesterday.

Martin: What happened?

Barton: I leaned over the fax machine, caught my tie in it and the next thing I knew I was in Cleveland.

Harley lived on Staten Island and commuted to his job in Manhattan. After a string of unfortunate incidents which resulted in him being late several times, he was rushing to work one morning when he saw the ferry already ten feet away from the dock.

Determined not to have to wait a half hour for the next boat and be late for work again, Harley ran as fast as he could, jumped the safety chain, dashed up the ramp and made a fantastic flying leap at the vessel. He just barely caught the edge of the deck and hung on by his fingernails until he managed to pull himself on board to the applause of hundreds of fellow commuters.

Harley waved and took a slight bow towards his admirers. One of them stepped up, shook his hand and said, "Gee pal, that was really spectacular but you should have waited a few seconds...we're just coming in."

My rise to the top was through sheer ability and inheritance.

—Malcolm Forbes

A molehill man is a pseudo-busy executive who comes to work at 9 a.m. and finds a molehill on his desk. He has until 5 p.m. to make the molehill into a mountain. An accomplished molehill man will often have his mountain finished before lunch.

—Fred Allen

A rnie: My girlfriend lost her job.

Barney: What kind of work did she do?

Arnie: She was a proofreader in the M&Ms factory.

Barney: What happened?

Arnie: She kept throwing out all the 'W's.'

Did you hear the one about the elephant at the computer store?

He wanted a model with lots of memory but no mouse.

Conglomerates are known by the companies they keep.

I've got a job...looking for one. I've been out of work so long I forgot what kind of work I'm out of.

—Robin Harris

Management: An organization that makes it difficult for other people to work.

—Peter Drucker

SANTA & CO.

To: All employees

From: The Boss

Subject: Suggestion Box

I've just finished examining the contents of the office suggestion box. In the future, please be more specific. To wit: What kind of kite? Which lake?

Patient: Doc, remember how you told me to take some time off from my business, to take it easy for a while?

Doctor: I remember telling you that.

Patient: Could you tell me one more thing? How do I get my business back?

HO-HO-HO!

A door to door salesman decided to drop by the police station one Christmas season to ask if any of the officers might be interested in his line of toys.

As soon as he started his pitch, the desk sergeant held up his hand and said, "I'm sorry, you can't sell these toys without a license."

"So that's it," replied the salesman. "I knew I wasn't selling any but I didn't know the reason."

I don't want any yes-men around me.
I want everybody to tell me the truth,
even if it costs them their jobs.

—Samuel Goldwyn

In the computer world, hardware is anything you can hit with a hammer, software is what you can only curse at.

—Anonymous

Farnsworth: So are you going to hire that new secretary? I hear she's really gorgeous.

Brentwood: Yeah, but I don't know how smart she is.

Farnsworth: Oh? What do you mean?

Brentwood: Well, on her employment application where it says 'Sign here', she put 'Pisces.'

HO·HO·HO!

Late in the afternoon one Christmas Eve, the phone rang at the law firm of Grayson, Grayson, Grayson and Grayson.

"Hello, may I help you?"

"Yes, I'd like to talk to Mr. Grayson," said the man on the phone.

"I'm sorry. He's spending Christmas with his family in Vermont."

"All right, then...let me speak to Mr. Grayson."

"Mr. Grayson flew to Hawaii this morning for the holidays."

"Okay, I'll take it up with Mr. Grayson."

"He took off to do some last-minute Christmas shopping."

"All right, then connect me with Mr. Grayson."

"Speaking."

Time is money, especially overtime.

—Evan Esar

Anyone can do any amount of work
provided it isn't the work he is supposed
to be doing at that moment.

—Robert Benchley

The boss is so cheap that when you call in sick you have to use a 900 number.

Interviewer: I see your resume says you're 22. If we start you at the bottom of our company, what do you think you'll be in three years?

Interviewee: 25.

A salesman applying for a position was asked about his professional background. He said, "I've had back-to-back jobs. The first was a hush-hush job at Sing Sing. Then, from time to time I was a door-to-door salesman with a fifty-fifty commission selling wall-to-wall carpeting day to day in Walla Walla."

"And would you say you were successful in both occupations?" asked the interviewer.

"So-so."

"How many employees work here?"

"About half of them."

The trouble with the rat race is that even if you win, you're still a rat.

—Mark Twain

If a cluttered desk is an indication of a cluttered mind, what is indicated by an empty desk?

—Anonymous

HO-HO-HO!

Charlie walked in the door carrying a fruitcake.

"The good news, Honey, is that I got a Christmas bonus. The bad news is, it's edible."

Then there was the secretary who could write shorthand, but it takes her longer.

Business Cards

IN A RESTAURANT WINDOW:
DON'T STAND OUTSIDE AND BE MISERABLE.
COME INSIDE AND BE FED UP.

IN A DELI:
PROTECT YOUR BAGELS. PUT LOX ON THEM.

TWO SPECIALISTS, A PSYCHIATRIST AND A
PROCTOLOGIST, TEAMED UP FOR A MEDICAL
PRACTICE. THEIR BUSINESS CARD READS:
ODDS AND ENDS.

ONE OF THE FEW COMPANIES THAT SPECIALIZES
IN CLEANING UP NUCLEAR WASTE SPILLS CALLS
ITSELF:
THE FASTEST RELIEF KNOWN
FOR ATOMIC ACHE!

HERE'S SANTA'S PERSONAL FAVORITE,
SEEN IN A PET STORE WINDOW:
MERRY CHRISTMAS AND A YAPPY NEW YEAR!

The computer is down. I hope it's

something serious.

—Stanton Delaplane

Brinkman: I'd like to offer you the job as my new accountant. Will you accept?

Finster: Certainly, sir. May I inquire as to what my starting salary is?

Brinkman: $125,000 a year.

Finster: $125,000 a year!?! If you don't mind me asking, Mr. Brinkman, how can such a small business afford to pay that kind of money?

Brinkman: Hey, you're my new accountant. That's your worry.

The best thing about telling a clean joke at the office is that there's a very good chance no one has ever heard it.

Office Terminology

When you make a mistake you're called an "imbecile."

When the boss makes a mistake he's "only human."

When you come in late you're "undependable."

When the boss comes in late he's "pacing himself."

If you miss a deadline you're "irresponsible."

If the boss misses a deadline he's "thorough."

When you're out of the office you're "dodging your work."

When the boss is out of the office he's "on business."

When you take a long lunch you're "goofing off on company time."

When the boss takes a long lunch he's "entertaining clients."

When you perform a task singlehandedly with complete originality and creativity you "lack team spirit."

When the boss does the same thing it shows "initiative."

Work is accomplished by those employees who have not yet reached their level of incompetence.

—Laurence J. Peter

HO-HO-HO!

At the Christmas party, the boss had quite a few under his belt to ward off the winter's night when he got to talking with young Griswold from the stockroom.

"Listen kid, I know that this year's pay cuts have everyone around here upset but I can tell you that having a million bucks doesn't bring happiness."

Griswold nodded sympathetically until the boss added, "Look at me...I've got ten million and I'm no happier than when I had nine million."

Riding the "El" train in Philadelphia, two commuters struck up a conversation.

"I have four children," said one man proudly.

"Oh my, I wish I had four children," sighed the other.

"Don't you have any children?" his new acquaintance asked.

"Yeah, eight."

A decision is what a man makes when he can't find anybody to serve on a committee.

—Fletcher Knebel

Boss Busters

People love to tell jokes about their boss. It's a natural, healthy venting of workplace frustration. Why, I've even overheard the elves telling jokes about me...those are the ones who now have the job of cleaning the reindeer pen...Ho Ho Ho! Enjoy these boss busters but be careful not to wind up on your boss' "naughty" list...

Some people climb the ladder of success. My boss walked under it.

Q: Why does the boss only get half-hour lunch breaks?

A: So the company doesn't have to retrain him

Sound planning goes into every one of the boss' sales meetings...a lot of sound and very little planning.

My boss' past endeavors have earned him quite a following—private detectives, ex-wives, creditors...

The boss shorted out his computer again. He still hasn't learned that you don't have to lick the stamps on e-mail.

My boss is so cheap, instead of cards he sends out a Christmas chain letter.

The boss' idea of a multimedia presentation is one with an overhead projector and an underhanded sales pitch.

I wouldn't want to say the boss is cheap. He's just generosity-challenged.

The boss put on so much weight over the holidays that now, when he goes into his office, he has to make two trips.

He had insomnia so bad that he couldn't sleep while working.

—Arthur "Bugs" Baer

A baseball game is twice as much fun if

you're seeing it on the company's time.

—William C. Feather

After an hour of cigar chomping, back-slapping and martini-drinking, the millionaire businessman leaned across the table and said to his guest, "It's good to have lunch with you again, Senator...and to show my appreciation for your voting record on bills affecting my business interests, I'd like to give you an $80,000 Mercedes from my dealership."

"I can't accept that, man. It would be bribery," said the Senator.

"I could arrange to sell you the car for $50."

"In that case, I accept. In fact, for $50 apiece, I'll take two!"

When a salesman marries a saleswoman do they become sell-mates?

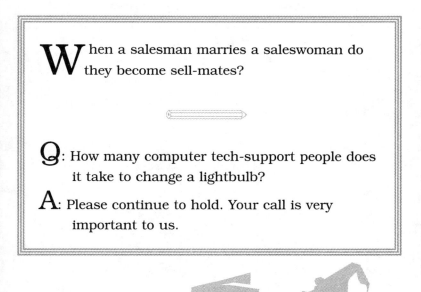

Q: How many computer tech-support people does it take to change a lightbulb?

A: Please continue to hold. Your call is very important to us.

There is no monument dedicated to the memory of a committee.

—Lester J. Pourciau

*If economists were any good at business,
they would be rich men instead of
advisers to rich men.*

—Kirk Kerkorian

HO-HO-HO!

Q: What did one of Santa's elves put on the Internet?

A: A gnome page

Maybe you've heard about the pit bull that was crossed with a computer.

Its bark was worse than its megabyte.

T he CEO left his office building and was attacked by two thugs in the firm's parking lot. He put up a valiant effort but, finally, was subdued. He surrendered the two dollars that were in his wallet.

"You fought that hard for a measly two bucks?" asked one of the muggers.

"Well," replied the CEO, "I thought you were after the thousand dollars I have in my shoe."

When it comes to work, there are many who will stop at nothing.

—Bob Phillips

The brain is a wonderful organ; it starts working the moment you get up in the morning and does not stop until you get into the office.

—Robert Frost

Want to make a pain in the neck of yourself? The next time you're on an office elevator continually ask, "Are we there yet?"

A couple of burglars were trapped on the 13th floor of an office building which they were trying to rob.

One says to the other, "Jump!"

The other burglar says, "I can't. I'm too scared!"

The first one says, "Oh, for crying out loud! This is no time to be superstitious!"

Randy: I just got a great new secretary.

Andy: Does she take shorthand?

Randy: No.

Andy: Does she know how to file?

Randy: No.

Andy: Well then, is she a good typist?

Randy: No, but she erases 65 words a minute.

There are an enormous number of managers who have retired on the job.

—Peter Drucker

HO-HO-HO!

A guy goes into his dentist's office complaining of a sore mouth.

The dentist examines him and exclaims, "My gosh. That plate I installed in your mouth three months ago is almost completely corroded! What in the devil have you been eating?"

The guy answers, "The only thing I can think of is a new sauce that my wife cooked up a couple of months ago. She calls it Hollandaise sauce...and, Doc, is it awesome! I've never tasted anything so delicious. I've been putting it on everything...meat, fish, vegetables."

"That's the problem," says the dentist. "One of the primary ingredients of Hollandaise sauce is lemon juice which is highly corrosive...I'm going to have to make you a new upper plate and this time I'll make it out of chrome."

"Why chrome, Doc?"

"Simple," responds the dentist. "Everyone knows that there's no plate like chrome for the Hollandaise!"

T wo secretaries were discussing the office computer technician while on a break.

"Why's he so depressed?" asked one.

"Well I asked him that very question and he explained that it's because he upgraded from Girlfriend 1.0 to Wife 1.0 last year," replied the other secretary.

"So why does that make him sad?"

"Because now he says he's having trouble running other applications such as Poker Night 1.05 and Fishing Trip 3.1."

Here's a business tip for you. For a quick energy boost, nothing beats having the boss walk into your office.

—Leona Enochs

If you get to 35 and your job still involves
wearing a name tag, you've probably
made a serious vocational error.

—Dennis Miller

HO-HO-HO!

Here's one that proves Santa must have a sense of humor:

Q: Why is Christmas just like a day at the office?

A: You do all the work and the fat guy with the suit gets all the credit.

"**H**ow was your day, honey?" Waldo's wife asked.

"Great," said Waldo. "My boss advised me to look at the big picture so I went to the movies!"

On his way out of the office late Christmas Eve, Crumstead, the junior clerk in the payroll office, spotted the CEO of the company standing by the document shredder. The exec was pressing buttons and mumbling some very un-Christmaslike sentiments. As the CEO began to kick the machine, Crumstead strolled over and said, "Let me help you, sir. You see, the paper goes in like this and then you just press the 'start' button."

"Fine, fine, young man," said the CEO as the paper was sucked into the shredder. "I'll just need one copy."

Never work before breakfast; if you have to work before breakfast, eat your breakfast first.

—Josh Billings

Few great men could pass Personnel.

—Paul Goodman

Gustafson fancied himself quite a wit. Since he had twenty people working for him, he always had a captive audience on which to inflict his tired, worn-out jokes.

One day he told a particularly awful joke to his staff and everyone laughed...that is, everyone but Mr. Meekley, the mild-mannered shipping clerk.

Not laughing at the boss' jokes was unheard of so Gustsafson challenged the little fellow.

"What's the matter, Meekley? Why didn't you laugh at my joke?"

"Three reasons, sir," replied the soft-spoken clerk. "Number one, it wasn't funny. Number two, it was in very bad taste. And number three, I'm retiring tomorrow."

The traveling salesman's car broke down on a rural road. He knocked on the door of the proverbial farmhouse and asked if he could be put up for the night.

"Sure," the farmer answered, "but I have an 18-year-old daughter...and you've got to stay away from her."

The salesman looked at the daughter standing behind the old farmer and saw the most beautiful woman his eyes had ever beheld. She was gorgeous, absolutely stunning...but he needed lodging for the night so he agreed to the farmer's condition.

It was a very dark night and, in the country quiet, the farmer slept soundly.

The next morning, the salesman was up, dressed and had already called for a tow truck by the time the farmer arose. He thanked his host and left to meet the truck where his car had broken down.

Back at his farmhouse, the old farmer squinted suspiciously at his beautiful daughter and said, "Did the salesman stay away from you like he promised?"

"Of course he did, Pa," replied the wide-eyed ingenue. "After all, this is a joke book by Santa."

I lost my job. I didn't lose it...I know where it is...It's just that when I go there, someone else is doing it.

—Bobcat Goldthwaite

Boss: You should have been here at eight o'clock.

Secretary: Why? What happened?

Then there's the employee who always gives the company an honest day's work. Of course, it takes him a week to do it.

A woman riding on a crowded commuter train couldn't stand the decidedly nasty smell of the man standing beside her.

"Excuse me, sir," she said in a mannerly way, "but I think your deodorant has failed."

The man responded, "It must be yours, lady. I'm not wearing any."

And then there was the entrepreneur who opened a school for horseback riding. Unfortunately, his business fell off.

One man's pay increase is another man's price increase.

—Harold Wilson

There is something wrong with my eyesight. I can't see going to work.

—Teddy Bergeron

HO-HO-HO!

Just before Christmas, there were an honest politician, a kind boss and Santa Claus traveling in an elevator. As the doors opened, they noticed a five dollar bill lying on the floor. Which one picked it up?

Santa Claus, of course. The other two don't exist.

Q: What do you get when a Macintosh falls off a desk?

A: Apple turnover

Smith had a heart attack and passed away at his desk.

Naturally, the rest of the office was grief-stricken but none more so than the boss who realized he had been pushing Smith too hard on the Johnson report.

A few days later, after failing to locate the whereabouts of the Johnson file, the boss went to a psychic and asked her to try and contact Smith in the Great Beyond. The psychic agreed to try, rubbed her crystal ball and, indeed, did manage to get in touch with Smith's spirit.

Nervous, the boss asked, "So Smith, how is it where you are?"

"A heck of a lot better than at the office," came the reply.

"Heh-heh, yes I guess so," responded the boss, glad that Smith was happy. "Say, I was wondering before you go back to enjoying heaven if you could tell me where the Johnson report is?"

"It's in my third drawer," the disembodied voice shot back. "And who said anything about heaven?"

Hard work never killed anybody, but why take a chance?

—Charlie McCarthy (Edgar Bergen)

"Do you know the motto of our firm?" asked the boss of his new office clerk.

"Sure it's 'Push'," answered the clerk.

"Whatever gave you that idea?" questioned the boss.

"I noticed it on the door when I came in."

Boss: You're supposed to answer the phone when it rings.

Secretary: But most of the time it's for you.

The World's *Cleanest* Traveling Salesman Joke…

Tom went to Chicago to see his old buddy, Steve, who still ran the little corner grocery store that his father started a half-century ago.

Stepping into the store, Steve shook hands with his friend and they brought each other up to date. At one point, Tom became distracted as he saw that the shelves of the store were all filled with soap. As Tom was shown around the place, he couldn't help but notice that the stockroom was filled with soap and, out back, there was a 50 foot storage trailer filled with soap.

"Gee, pal," said Tom shaking his head. "You sure do sell a lot of soap here!"

"Nah, not really," replied Steve. "But the guy who sold it to me…brother, could he sell soap!"

I work like a horse, but only when my boss rides me.

—Henny Youngman

Don't steal; thou'lt never thus compete successfully in business. Cheat.

—Ambrose Bierce

In an old New England mill town, the residents got together to figure out how to use the abandoned factory buildings to boost the town's economy.

"I have an idea," said a bright young lad. "Germans love to travel with their dogs but most American lodgings don't allow them. Why not turn the buildings into canine hotels?"

The proposal won approval by a narrow margin and the factories were converted into pooch accommodations.

A few months later, one of the people who had opposed the plan returned home from a long trip and happened to ask the young lad how the plan was going.

"Can't you hear?" asked the lad, cupping his hand to his ear. "The mills are alive with the hounds of Munich."

HO·HO·HO!

Boss: Who told you that just because I lost my head and kissed you at the office Christmas party that you didn't have to do any work around here?

Secretary: My lawyer.

The CEO of the Fisbin Toy Company told his staff, "I've got good news and bad news...The good news is that our jigsaw puzzles are outselling every other product we make. The bad news is, our business is going to pieces."

A genius is one who can do anything except make a living.

—Joey Adams

Working Knowledge

The reason they call it "take-home" pay is because there's nowhere else you can go with it.

Yesterday is experience, tomorrow is hope, today is getting from one to the other.

Give a man food, and he can eat for a day. Give a man a job, and he can only eat for 30 minutes on break.

If you're looking to kill time, remember that a committee is a perfect weapon.

Experience is something you don't get until just after you need it.

If your work speaks for itself, don't interrupt.

The reason they call it "Form 1040" is that for every $50 you earn, you get ten and the IRS gets forty.

You know you're in trouble when your job is re-classified from "entry level" to "exit level."

A guy spotted a lamp by the side of the road. He rubbed it and a genie appeared.

"I will grant you one wish," said the genie.

The guy thought for a second and then said, "I want a terrific job...one that no man has ever succeeded at or attempted to do."

Poooof!

The genie turned him into a housewife.

Work is the greatest thing in the world,

so we should always save some of it

for tomorrow.

—Don Herold

A computer programmer dies and is met by St. Peter at the pearly gates. St. Peter gives the programmer the option of spending eternity in Heaven or Hell.

The programmer says, "Is it possible to take a quick look at both places before I make up my mind?"

St. Peter says, "Why, of course."

They take a gander at Hell first. Oddly, Hell seems to be a heckuva place...one big party with good food, drink and great atmosphere.

Then St. Peter and the programmer visit Heaven. It's serene to say the least. There are angels sitting on clouds, people in white robes and a general aura of peace, but it doesn't appear to be nearly as much fun as Hell.

The programmer tells St. Peter he prefers Hell. St. Peter grants him his wish and off to Hell the programmer goes.

The computer geek is sorely disappointed to find out that Hell isn't what he thought it was. Hell turns out to be one big ball of fire with people screaming at the top of their lungs, the sound of glass breaking everywhere...in general one eternal nightmare.

The programmer registers a complaint with Satan himself.

"What's the problem?" asks Satan.

The programmer responds, "I chose to go to Hell rather than Heaven because it looked like it was a terrific place to have a good time, but this is nothing like I was shown."

Satan grins demonically and says, "Aha! That's because you only saw the demo."

A businessman needs three umbrellas...one to leave at the office, one to leave at home, and one to leave on the train.

—Paul Dickson

Early to rise and early to bed makes a
male healthy and wealthy and dead.

—James Thurber

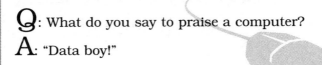

Q: What do you say to praise a computer?
A: "Data boy!"

And then there was the computer that died of a terminal illness.

Boss: That's it! I've had enough. You're fired!

Employee: Fired? I always thought slaves were sold.

The CEO called the new employee in for his evaluation.

"Congratulations, Johnson. Congratulations. You've set a company record."

"Really, sir? How?"

"You've only been with us two weeks and already you're a month behind in your work."

Boss: I never want you to repeat office gossip.

Secretary: What else is there to do with it?

I think of my boss as a father figure. That really irritates her.

—Mary Jo Crowley

A disheveled young fellow ambled into the office of a car agency's sales manager. He took one look at the manager and mumbled, "I guess you don't want to buy any life insurance," and he turned away.

"Hold on, son!" called the manager. "I've been in sales for 40 years and I have to say that I have never seen a worse sales approach. But I like you, boy, and I'm going to help—sort of take you under my wing so to speak. The first thing you've got to do is gain confidence and to help you out, I want you to write me up a one million dollar policy.

As soon as the insurance novice had his signature on the dotted line, he began to leave but the manager called him back.

"Hold on, son. Now that you've got confidence, you've got to learn the tricks of the trade."

"Oh, yes, sir. The tricks of the trade are very important," replied the young insurance agent. "The one I just used on you is designed especially for sales managers."

HO-HO-HO!

Q: How would you fire Santa?

A: Give him the sack.

Q: What do you call a bunch of grandmasters of chess bragging about their games in the lobby of an office building?

A: Chess nuts boasting in an open foyer

The biggest energy crisis in America is Monday morning.

—Terence Tackett

Bytes of Humor

Q: Where do computers go on vacation?
A: To the Big Apple

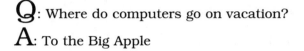

Q: What's the best way to park a computer?
A: You back it up.

Q: What did the football punter do to the computer?
A: He booted it up.

Q: What happens when you cross a computer with an elephant?
A: You get loads of memory.

T om and Tim were on their coffee break discussing investments.

Tom: I dialed one of those 900 numbers that give you financial advice.

Tim: What did they tell you?

Tom: They advised me not to call 900 numbers.

SANTA & CO.

Our experts describe you as an appallingly dull fellow: unimaginative, timid, lacking in initiative, spineless, easily dominated, no sense of humor, tedious company, and irrepressibly drab and awful. And whereas in most professions, these would be considerable drawbacks, in chartered accountancy, they're a positive boon!

—John Cleese

All work and no play makes Jack a dull boy...and Jill a wealthy widow.

—Evan Esar

Williams: I have to ask to be excused from jury duty, your honor. It's our busy season and I can't afford to be away from the office.

Judge: Oh, so you're one of those businessmen who thinks the company can't get along without you?

Williams: No, your honor. *I* know they can get along without me. I just can't afford for *them* to find out.

Melvin: Why do you think your business failed?

Herman: Too much was spent on advertising.

Melvin: You never spent a penny on ads.

Herman: No, but my competitor did.

Down in the canyons of Wall Street, a fabulously wealthy stockbroker passed a bedraggled beggar dressed in rags.

"Please, sir, may I trouble you for a dollar so that I might get a bite to eat?" pleaded the beggar.

"You poor fellow," said the stockbroker. "Listen. Come with me and I'll buy you a drink."

"Actually, sir, I don't drink, but I would like a bite to eat."

"Here, my good man. Take one of my special stock of Cuban cigars," urged the broker.

"Sorry, sir," said the bum. "I don't smoke."

"Well, listen then. Come with me down to Atlantic City. I'll stake you in the casino and you might win enough to get your life back on track."

"I can't do that, sir. I don't gamble, but I would still like a bite to eat."

"You want to eat?" asked the stockbroker. "Very well, come home with me and have dinner with us."

"That's very kind of you, sir. Thank you."

"Not at all," replied the broker. "I just want my wife to see what happens to a man who doesn't drink, smoke or gamble!"

Every morning I get up and look through the Forbes list of the richest people in America. If I'm not there, I go to work.

—Robert Orben

There once was a company that manufactured doorbells but it went out of business. All of its salespeople worked door-to-door, so when they rang, people who needed the product didn't know they were there.

Secretary: I can do fifty words a minute.

Boss: Really? Is that typing or shorthand?

Secretary: Reading.

A n enterprising young man started his own business. He leased a posh top-floor office in the big city. The first day he was in the office he was sitting at the desk when he saw another guy come into the reception room. Trying to look as executively important as possible, the entrepreneur picked up the telephone and got into a one-way big deal business conversation. After throwing around seven-figure digits for the make-believe deal, he hung up the phone and inquired of the visitor, "What can I do for you?"

The guy answered, "I've come to install your phone."

A verbal contract isn't worth the paper it's printed on.

—Samuel Goldwyn

Asking if computers can think is like asking if submarines can swim.

—Anonymous

HO·HO·HO!

While Christmas shopping, Mrs. Bindlemeyer maxed out her credit cards so she decided to drop by her husband's office to pick up some cash.

When she walked in unexpectedly, she found the secretary sitting on Mr. Bindlemeyer's lap, taking dictation.

Without missing a beat, the husband continued, "And in conclusion, gentlemen, expense reduction program or no expense reduction program, this office can no longer continue to operate with just one chair."

Razz-umes

His resume says he served on a disciplinary board. We looked it up...turns out they made him walk the plank.

His resume says he made excellent grades at Harvard. We looked it up...turns out he drove a bulldozer in the school parking lot.

His resume says he used to be a professional diver. We looked it up...turns out he used to be a boxer.

His resume says that at his last job he was known for having the Midas touch. We looked it up...turns out he installed mufflers.

His resume says he has experience in oil and gas. We looked it up...turns out he was a fry cook at Taco Bell.

His resume says he spent five years taking it off for Chippendale's. We looked it up...turns out he was a furniture stripper.

*Adults are always asking little kids what
they want to be when they grow up
because they're looking for ideas.*

—Paula Poundstone

Burt: How come you dropped out of computer school?

Curt: I just couldn't hack the program.

Q: What do you get if you cross Bugs Bunny with computer software?

A: A rabbit with floppy ears

A businessman went to a hunting lodge and, accompanied by a dog named Salesman, bagged a record number of birds.

The next year he returned and asked for Salesman once again. Again, a record number of birds.

The third year he was back again, anticipating another banner hunting trip with Salesman but the lodge manager said, "The hound ain't no good anymore."

"What happened!" asked the businessman. "Was he injured?"

"No," the manager replied. "Some danged fool came down here and called him 'Sales Manager' for a week instead of Salesman. Now all he does it sit on his tail and bark."

The world is full of willing people...some willing to work, the rest willing to let them.

—Robert Frost

Work fast—not half fast.

—Graffiti

T he boss' new secretary didn't know much
 about computers. Last summer she blew out
three monitors trying to put screens on Windows.

T wo executives are lunching at a swank
 restaurant but one seems preoccupied.

"What's wrong, Kirk?" asked Mike.

"Oh, it's my secretary. I think I'm going to have
to fire her. She keeps asking me how to spell the
simplest words."

"Gee, that's a shame," said Mike. "That can
really be annoying."

"Annoying nothing...it's embarrassing saying 'I
don't know' all the time!"